Life of the Mind

Life of the Mind

Poems by

Julia Caroline Knowlton

Cover design by Nell Ruby, Professor of Art, Agnes Scott College
Cover image and author photo by Julia Caroline Knowlton

ISBN: 978-1-63980-394-1

Kelsay Books
502 South 1040 East, A-119
American Fork, Utah 84003
Kelsaybooks.com

for

everyone I love

L'amour le plus exclusif pour une personne
[. . .] est l'amour d'autre chose.

The most exclusive love for a person
[. . .] is the love of something else.
—Marcel Proust

[. . .]   sick with desire
And fastened to a dying animal
[My heart] knows not what it is. . . .
—W.B. Yeats
Sailing to Byzantium

Acknowledgments

The author gratefully acknowledges the editors of the following publications in which the following individual poems appeared (some in earlier drafts):

Amethyst Review: "To a Pigeon in Paris"

Eunoia Review: "To My Former Husband"

Neologism: "Life of the Mind," "When We Make Love," "On Painting"

One Art: "Meditation in Winter," "Learning Italian," "Letter Home," "Alone in Verona," "Getting Older," "Meditation"

Peacock: "To the Next Man I Will Love"

Roanoke Review: "Above and Below," "Postcard from Paris"

Rust and Moth: "My Period at Fifty"

Third Wednesday: "Everything I Need"

tiny wren lit: "L'Adieu"

Trouvaille Review: "A Picture in Spring"

Contents

L'Adieu

It was August in Georgia
when sick heat turns illicit.

I called the question of us—
your slow answer was no.

In our humid night the lilies'
red stigmas began to sway

but the yellow bowl of lemons
had no possible subtext.

You blew out the wick of us.
I cleared all the dishes away.

Still Life

lying alone in my bed of bone
like a fever I feel
the steady heat of our lies

late in the day
I buy myself lilies
to bury in a crystal vase

I take comfort arranging
their perfume in wet clarity so pure
my new picture with no error to erase

Meditation in Winter

I draw an angel halo on paper,
believing only in paper

not the gold shape itself.
I light candles with a red-hot match.

I sing a bitter song or sweet,
peel apples into butter and taste the past.

I write faint words, wash a dish.
Enter crying darkness coming at last.

My Period at Fifty

Surprise—a bright red smear
on white tissue.

The candied cherry
at the bottom of the sundae.

A painted clown's nose.

A cardinal perched alone in snow.

Two Gingko Trees

Every year in December
this cold blinding sight.

In one fell swoop, all the leaves fall.

The duet suddenly weeps—
a deep pour of gold

against cobalt sky,
pure and just as any darkening.

Thousands of leaves become
carpets of light—

vanishing excess, abundance in absence.

Life of the Mind

By nature, it is a wild thing. Its ocean waves
rove violet, leaves bud red, flowers dry & die.

It is a quest having neither sense nor witness,
seeking gold with nothing to find. Too often

it must be otherwise: an awareness tamed,
ever observed by words. An animal prancing

in a harness, obeying to survive.
I try breaking free, eating seed, fruit & rind.

Within this line I fly—hard seed, fruit & rind.

Getting Older

I am becoming a dappled thing.
Silver threads my hair,
dark spots dot my body
like a speckled egg.

Floaters cloud my vision,
meandering opaque grey
in the tiny sky of my eyes.
My ears ring with a song of demise.

A great poet (immortal)
once praised this color palette—
mottled, rose-stippled,
time's upstream beauty of change.

I can seed a pieced field
with one odd word.
I feed on instinct, on dream.
I am spare and strange.

Everything I Need

I have an unread book
made of soft cotton,
leather and thread.

I have the black ink
of unwritten words,
unscented white wax,
smoky candle wicks.

Every day I have a sky
wider and wilder
than any idea of sky,

my very own broken stone
of love, and keys of memory
made out of cloud.

To My Former Husband

So many years after our end,
I hand you this map. Its fantom land

holds the stone of our wrongdoing.
Roads bending too late, too soon.

Will you kiss the last cloud?
I stir us with my wooden spoon.

To the Next Man I Will Love

Why would I even think of you?

you with no name,
you with your hair of stone.

Yet I keep preparing myself—

eating my golden apples,
washing my faraway feet.

When We Make Love

When we make love, just what kind of love
are we making; the kind where you wear black

and I wear white, and we float near blue flowers
in a sky, in a painting? Or the kind where we walk

down a city street in wool coats, crunching autumn
leaves underfoot, then go our separate ways?

I know nothing when your force washes through me.
I know that all emotion is mere water, falling in more water.

Who can say what hidden stones might be moved.
Who can say what wet ground might stay.

Eternal Idol

after Rodin

Lips eclipse in cool resistance of stone.
His insistence silenced by the enigma

of her curves. As she bends to his need,
the arc of her heart surpasses it. She feels

his questions enter and become her own.
This is their communion beyond his animal grasp.

Her eyes close—
flowers unfurl with no promise of return.

A Picture in Spring

dogwood blossoms, white & pink
tiny dresses or ideas of prayer

too pure to be pure
too many poets call them stars

yet stars they are

innocence mute   without consciousness
little illustrations   floating in air

help me endure   help you endure

Meditation

March colors stain
perfumed air—

pink tulip magnolia,
ivory dogwood, fuchsia azalea.

Abundance blossoming
in a dark arch of rain.

Within this wet darkening
cries an unseen blessing.

In every hidden bird singing
dies my every word.

Learning Italian

I leave my Ohio English, native tongue,
its clip-clop sound of horse hooves

on a road, its plain words lined up like
birds on a wire or sliced fruit in a pan.

I learn *chiacchierare*—to chit chat—
admiring how the letters pirouette.

Pure music subsumes me—*alba, oro,
fruttivendolo, verdurivendolo.*

I fade *inamorata* into the wonder
of stone drapery and scrolls of violins.

Gold leaf frames an unseen poem,
an unknown home where I disappear.

Alone in Verona

I love you but did not invite you here.
I chose to come here alone
with mere impressions of us,

inner pictures winning out
over the star-crossed real.
In my mind are unseen frescoes,

emotion ground fine
into the plaster of thought—
burnt umber, blue, ochre of rose.

I love you but did not invite you here.
Why do I insist on this dizzying dream?
This lonely dizzying dream—

footpaths made of pink marble
scents of espresso & leather
the ancient ringing of bells

the iron lantern of exile
robed statues watching the dead
the dead cut out into little stars

speaking to everyone everywhere here

Postcard from Paris

I bring my pain here, to feel it.
To walk on apple-sized cobblestones.
How they soothe. And the food,
and the *chocolat chaud.*

Music everywhere:
jazz, solo cello and rap.
In summer dusk, in the dark pink air,
the swallows tell each other

once again what they know.
Then the toy boat vendor
packs up his cart
in the Luxembourg garden.

Footsteps across grass.
There is no better color
than everyone falling silent.
Wish everyone were here.

Letter Home

Paris is a paintbox of love's dark mystery
and light. Its bridges and lanterns,
wrought iron balconies and pale rose moon
on the Seine—all transcend time
but not place, like a desire for someone
you have never met. I was lovesick
for this place before I ever came here.
Like any *grand amour* this city will seduce you,
charm you, challenge and bewilder you.
Walk along the river, Breathe in the scent
of this city, a blend of expensive perfume,
butter, cigarette smoke and soot.
Watch the sun sink pink and low,
listen to creaking wooden shutters
concealing lives you cannot know.

Paris Bliss

All I want is to find my place
on a green velvet bench inside
La Contrescarpe, then make my way
toward the Pont Royal.

That sweep of stone over
the river, like a gown.
People wide-eyed.
Scent of Normandy butter in the air.

On Painting

After years of wanting
to try, I dared to try.
I opened tubes of color—
burnt umber, cerulean blue,

blood red, seafoam green.
I spread and whispered,
blotted, brushed and scraped,
swaying in a liquid dream.

It felt like betraying language
(that old marriage of black words
on a white page) in favor of color.
I felt like a wife taking a lover.

Cool touch of cotton canvas
stretched on a new bed!
Wet paint became my untold desire.
Now I come home to the poem

eager to leave again. I come
home to the poem with paint stains
on my skin, memories of the
color lover spattered in my mind.

To a Pigeon in Paris

Your iridescent breast
deep purple, silver, magenta fast flutter
shimmering mother of pearl
the same as shells in the sea

Your red-rimmed, dull stupid eye
senseless & opaque, your rhythmic
beak peck at bakery crumbs
regular as hands on a clock

Above all the single flap of your wings
against cold cobalt sky—
the supreme sound of it, one fast clap
too close to me, mere inches from my face

Thank you for your ordinary, ideal flight
allowing my tired heart instinct to alight

Above and Below

Paris, 2022

I remain too afraid to descend
into the Catacombs

to fathom the dark and damp
where skulls are piled in heart shapes

kept in place by stacks of tibias—
endless grey-white holes for eyes.

Holes never stop watching:
beggar, thief, prostitute, prince.

I will wait for shades and bones.
Better to stroll near the Seine

and toll of bells, tasting a hint
of ash in fresh air.

Now a rose window opening of rain.

About the Author

Julia Caroline Knowlton, PhD., MFA, is Professor of French at Agnes Scott College in Atlanta. The author of a memoir and three prior volumes of poetry, she was named a Georgia Author of the Year in 2018. Recognition for her work includes an Academy of American Poets Prize and inclusion in the 2022 Georgia Poetry in the Parks project. She regularly publishes her poetry in journals such as *One Art, Rust and Moth,* and *Neologism.* Now that her two children are adults, Julia enjoys traveling often to France and Italy and has recently begun making visual art.

www.ingramcontent.com/pod-product-compliance
Lightning Source LLC
Chambersburg PA
CBHW030816090426
42737CB00010B/1295